Contents

British Library Cataloguing in Publication Data

Martin, Paul
  Purnell's picture atlas.
  1. Atlases – Juvenile literature
  I. Title
  912   G1021

  ISBN 0-361-06695-3

Copyright © 1985 Purnell Publishers Limited
Published 1985 by Purnell Books, Paulton, Bristol BS18 5LQ,
a member of the BPCC group
Made and printed in Great Britain by Purnell
and Sons (Book Production) Limited, Paulton, Bristol
Phototypeset by Quadraset Limited

Illustrator: **Lynne Farmer (Linda Rogers Associates)**
Educational adviser: **Paul Martin**
Editor: **Janine Amos**
Designer: **Sarah Williams**

Purnell's
Picture Atlas

What is a Map?

Look at all these. They come from countries all over the world.

This book will tell you about some of those countries and show you where they are.

This is Kim.

Kim lives in this house.

If you looked straight down on Kim's house from an aeroplane, it would look like this.

Kim's house is in a street.

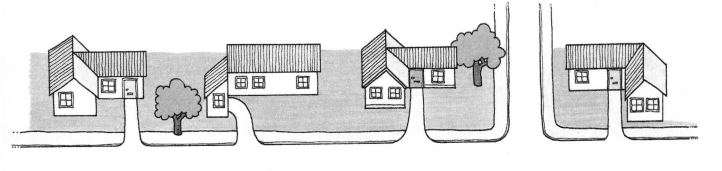

Looking straight down from an aeroplane, Kim's street would look like this.

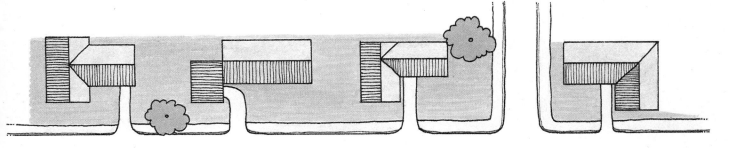

Kim's street is
in a city.

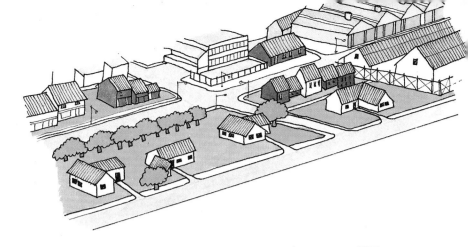

If your aeroplane were to fly
even higher and you looked
straight down on the city, it
would look like this.

Kim's city is in England. England is in the British Isles. If a
spaceman flying straight above the British Isles looked
down he would see that they looked like this.

If he drew the shape of the land he saw, it would be
called a map.

We can draw maps of all the countries in the world.

An atlas is a book full of maps. This atlas will tell you more about the different countries and help you find famous cities, rivers and buildings you may have heard of.

You will be able to find out which countries are hot and which are cold, where there are forests

and where there are deserts.

You will see where the different animals live,

and find out about the products

and industries of each country.

Let's begin by looking at a map of the whole world.

World Map

British Isles

There are five countries in the British Isles. Dairy farming is common. Industries include oil, steel, shipbuilding and motor cars.

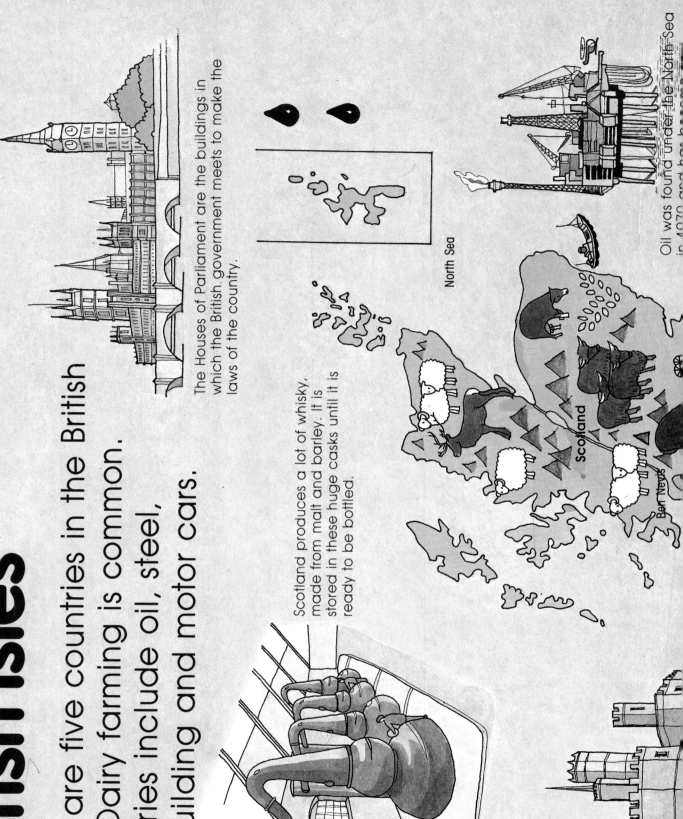

The Houses of Parliament are the buildings in which the British government meets to make the laws of the country.

North Sea

Oil was found under the North Sea in 1970 and has become

Scotland produces a lot of whisky, made from malt and barley. It is stored in these huge casks until it is ready to be bottled.

Scotland

Ben Nevis

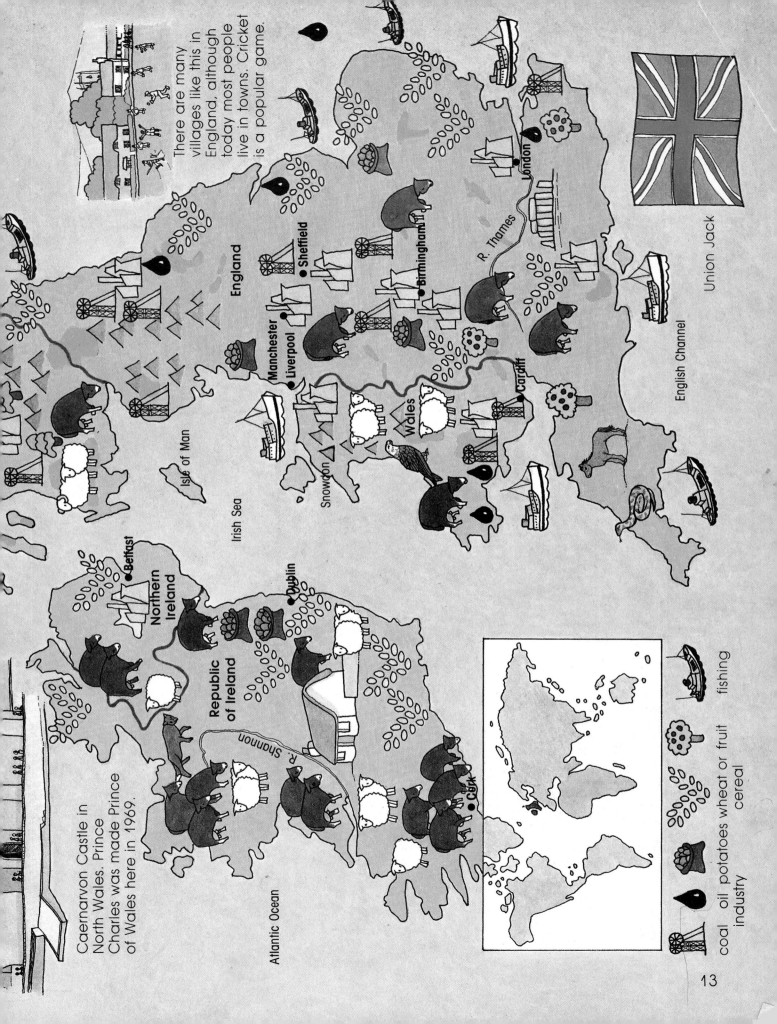

There are many villages like this in England, although today most people live in towns. Cricket is a popular game.

Union Jack

England

● Sheffield

● Manchester
Liverpool ●

Birmingham

London

R. Thames

English Channel

Isle of Man

Irish Sea

Snowdon

Wales

Cardiff

Caernarvon Castle in North Wales. Prince Charles was made Prince of Wales here in 1969.

● Belfast

Northern Ireland

● Dublin

Republic of Ireland

R. Shannon

● Cork

Atlantic Ocean

coal   oil   potatoes   wheat or fruit   fishing
      industry   cereal

13

Western Europe

Much of Europe's wealth depends on trade. Because of its long coastline, no part of Western Europe is far from a seaport. Its industries produce iron, steel and metal goods.

The Rhine is a busy waterway. The Rhine valley is famous for its castles and beautiful scenery.

In a few places in Portugal people still tread grapes to make wine.

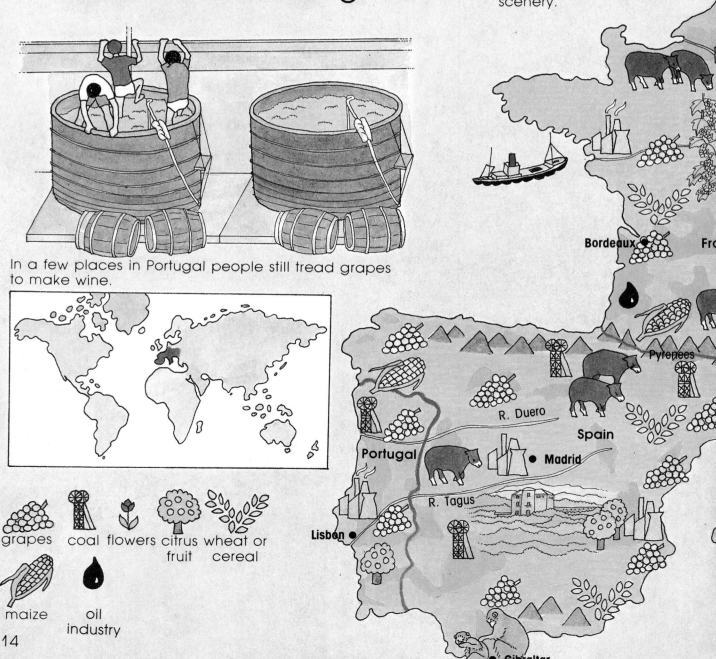

grapes   coal   flowers   citrus   wheat or
                              fruit   cereal

maize   oil
         industry

Bordeaux   Fr

Pyrenees

R. Duero

Spain

Portugal   Madrid

R. Tagus

Lisbon

Gibraltar

14

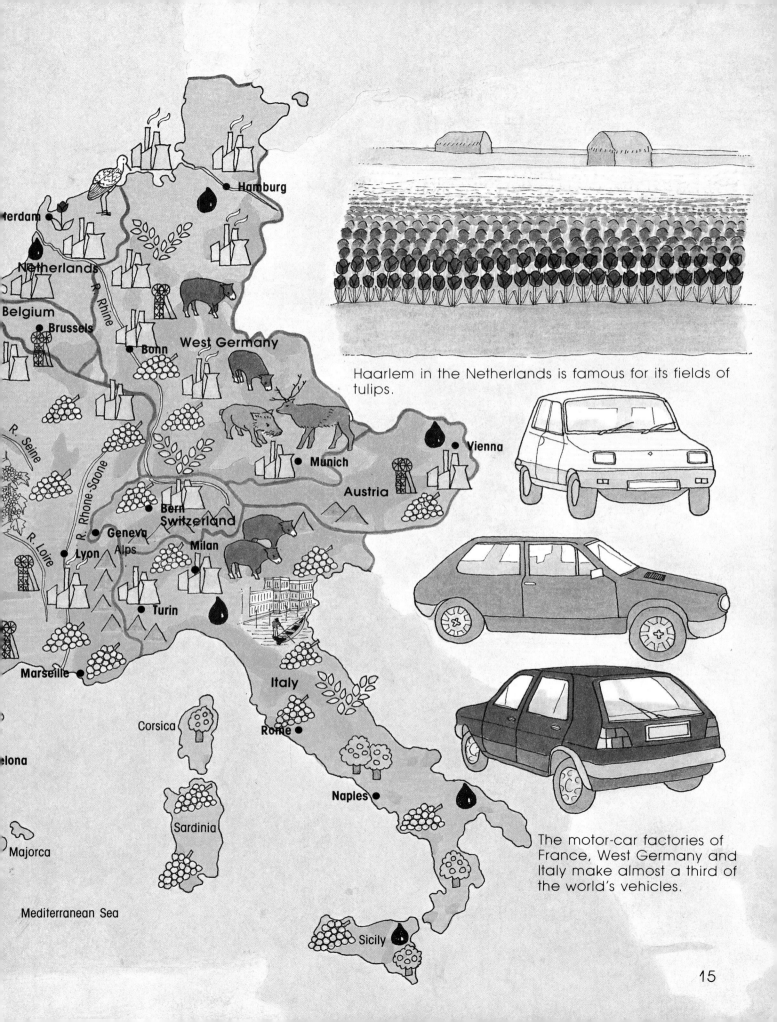

Hamburg

-terdam

Netherlands

Belgium

Brussels

Bonn

West Germany

R. Rhine

R. Seine

Munich

Vienna

Austria

Bern
Switzerland

Geneva

R. Rhone-Saone

Lyon

Alps

Milan

R. Loire

Turin

Marseille

Italy

Corsica

Rome

-elona

Sardinia

Naples

Majorca

Mediterranean Sea

Sicily

Haarlem in the Netherlands is famous for its fields of tulips.

The motor-car factories of France, West Germany and Italy make almost a third of the world's vehicles.

15

Eastern Europe

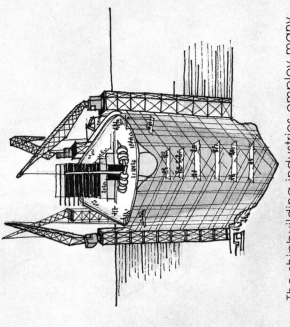

The shipbuilding industries employ many people in Poland and Greece.

wheat or cereal

cherries

grapes

potatoes

fruit

coal

citrus fruit

fishing

olives

Many people in Eastern Europe work on farms, but there are also big industrial centres. Most countries have warm summers and very cold winters. In Poland some rivers are frozen for several months of the year.

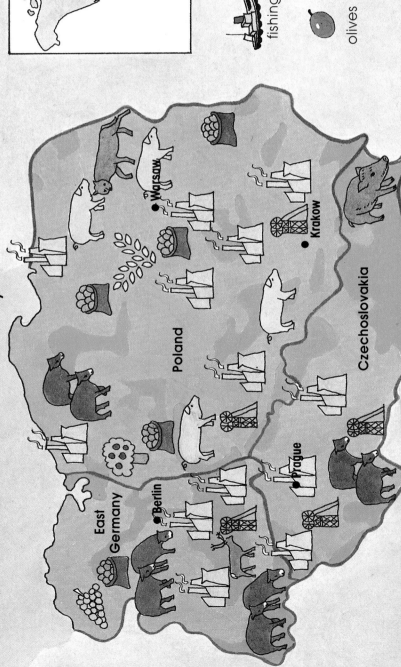

East Germany

Berlin

Warsaw

Poland

Krakow

Prague

Czechoslovakia

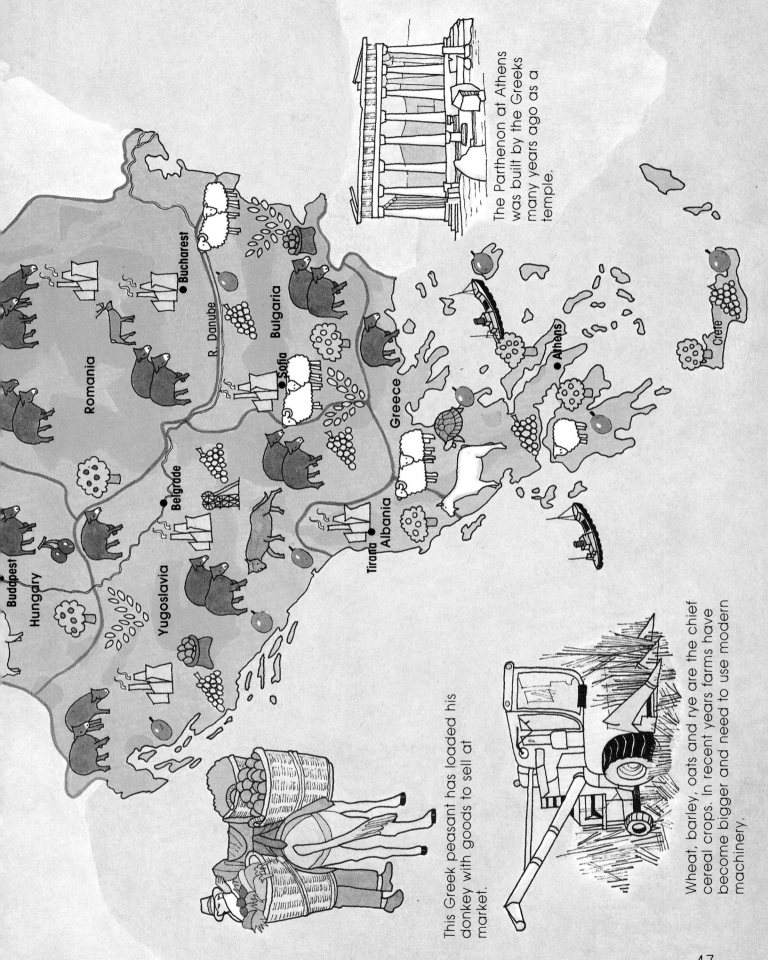

The Parthenon at Athens was built by the Greeks many years ago as a temple.

Bucharest

R. Danube

Bulgaria

Romania

Sofia

Belgrade

Greece

Athens

Crete

Albania

Tirana

Budapest

Hungary

Yugoslavia

This Greek peasant has loaded his donkey with goods to sell at market.

Wheat, barley, oats and rye are the chief cereal crops. In recent years farms have become bigger and need to use modern machinery.

Scandinavia and Iceland

There are four countries in Scandinavia. They are Norway, Sweden, Denmark and Finland. These countries are covered by forests and lakes. Iceland is an island about 1,000 km from Norway.

Along Norway's coast are many steep-sided valleys. They are called fjords.

Fishing is important, especially in Norway, and boats called trawlers are used to fish for cod and herring.

In Finland and Sweden there are great forests. The trees are used for making paper.

Hammerfest

forestry

fishing

wheat or
cereal

potatoes

iron ore

Finland

Helsinki

Stockholm

Sweden

Oslo

Norway

Copenhagen

Denmark

Reykjavik

19

U.S.S.R.

The U.S.S.R. is enormous! It is the biggest country in the world. Half the country is covered with forest. It is very cold in the north.

flag of U.S.S.R.

Leningrad

Kiev

Moscow

Gorky

Black Sea

R. Volga

Ural Mountains

Trans-Siberian Railway

Union of So

Oms

Caspian Sea

Caucasus Mountains

Tashkent

St. Basil's Cathedral, in Moscow, stands on the south side of Red Square which is often the scene of military parades.

In winter in the north it is so cold that the sea freezes. Boats like this are used to break the ice so that ships can enter the harbours.

Sport is popular in the U.S.S.R. Their gymnasts are well known all over the world.

...alist Republics

Lake Baykal

...sibirsk

Vladivostok

oil
industry

gold

wheat or cereal

coal

The Cossacks of the south are known for their horsemanship and also for their traditional Cossack dance.

21

Middle East

Much of the land here is hot desert where little grows because it is so dry. The main industry in the Middle East is the production of oil. Holes are drilled in the ground and the oil comes to the surface. Big tanker ships carry it abroad.

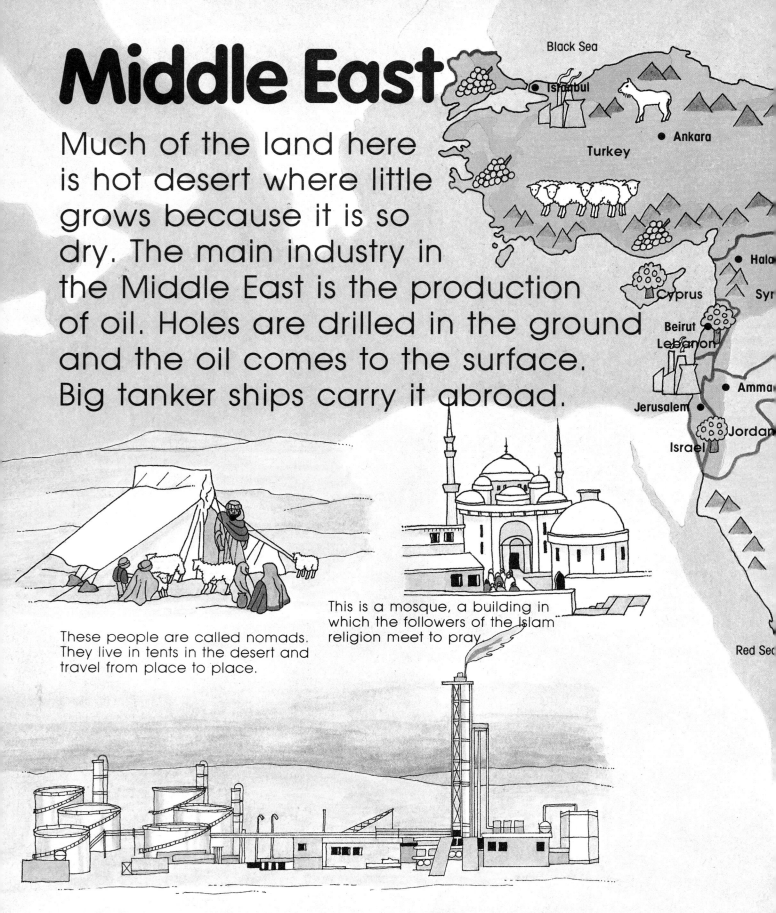

Black Sea

Istanbul

Ankara

Turkey

Cyprus

Hala

Syr

Beirut

Lebanon

Amma

Jerusalem

Israel

Jordan

Red Sea

These people are called nomads. They live in tents in the desert and travel from place to place.

This is a mosque, a building in which the followers of the Islam religion meet to pray

This is an oil well in the desert. Look at all the machinery needed to deal with the oil. Waste gas is burnt off and this makes a big flame.

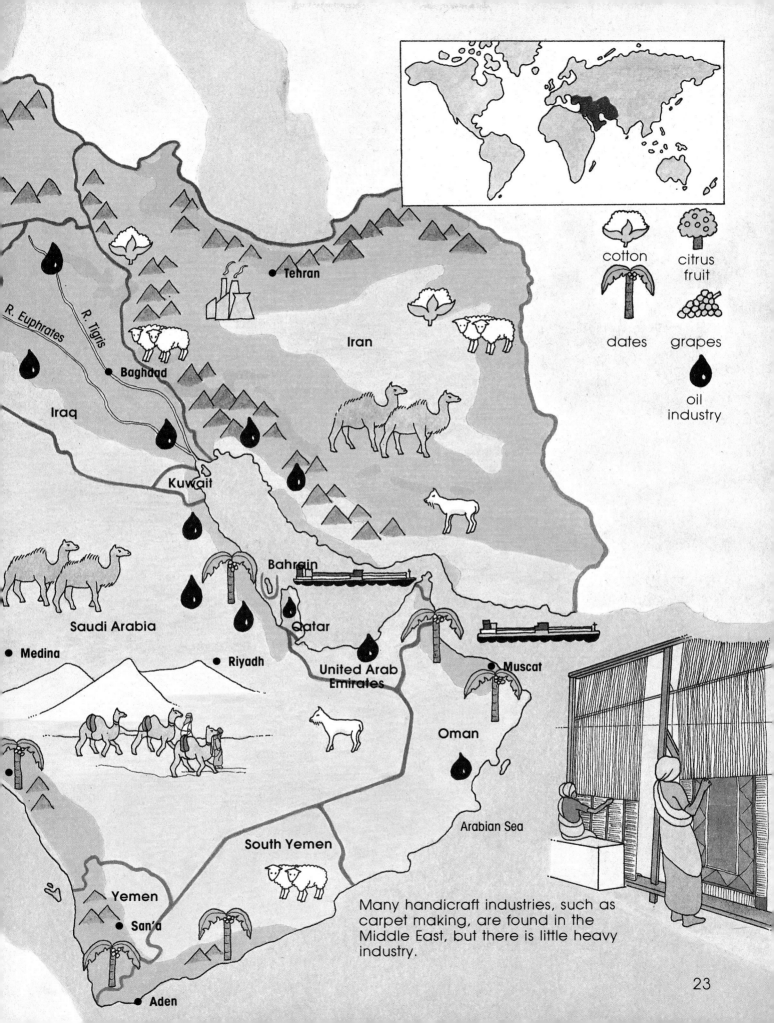

cotton

citrus fruit

dates

grapes

oil industry

R. Euphrates

R. Tigris

Tehran

Iran

Baghdad

Iraq

Kuwait

Saudi Arabia

Medina

Riyadh

Bahrain

Qatar

United Arab Emirates

Muscat

Oman

Arabian Sea

South Yemen

Yemen

San'a

Aden

Many handicraft industries, such as carpet making, are found in the Middle East, but there is little heavy industry.

Southern Asia

India is the largest country in Southern Asia. Many people in India are very poor. They work in the fields growing crops. The tea which they grow is sold all over the world. Industries are expanding in the large cities.

Cotton is a major industry. Indian cloth is beautifully dyed and printed, often by hand.

Many Indians bathe in the River Ganges which is their holy river.

Himalayas
Nepal
Mt. Everest
Delhi
Lahore
Islamabad
Kabul
Afghanistan
Indus River
Pakistan

Dacca

Calcutta

India

Ahmadabad

Bombay

Hyderabad

Bangalore Madras

Sri Lanka

Colombo

Arabian Sea

Indian Ocean

Sacred cows are allowed to wander wherever they like in India.

flag of India

tea   maize wheat or rice coal oil cotton
                cereal   industry

The Taj Mahal at Agra was built more than 300 years ago by an Indian ruler as the burial place and memorial for his wife.

Women pick the leaf buds from the tea plants and put them in their baskets. The young leaves are then chopped and dried to make tea.

25

Burma

Laos

Hanoi

oil rice rubber cotton sugar

Vientiane

Thailand

Rangoon

Bangkok

Kampuchea

Vietnam

Luzon

Manila

Philippin

Phnom Penh
Ho Chi Minh

South China Sea

Mind

Malaysia

Kuala
Lumpur

Singapore

Sumatra

Borneo

Sulawesi

Djakarta

Indonesia

Java

Indonesia has 167 volcanoes —
more than any other country.

South-east Asia

This area of the world is near the equator so it is hot and wet. There are many islands in South-east Asia and big areas of forest where lots of animals live.

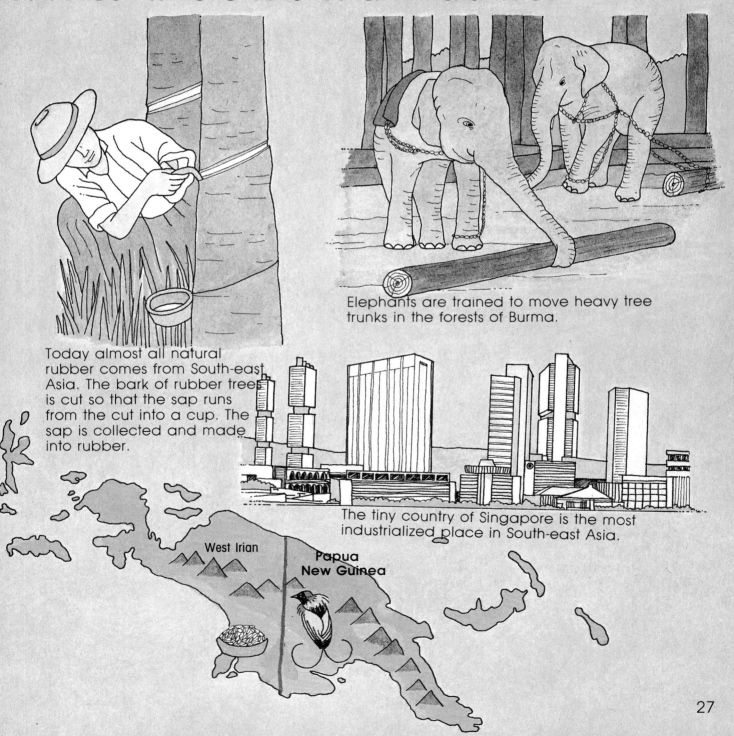

Elephants are trained to move heavy tree trunks in the forests of Burma.

Today almost all natural rubber comes from South-east Asia. The bark of rubber trees is cut so that the sap runs from the cut into a cup. The sap is collected and made into rubber.

The tiny country of Singapore is the most industrialized place in South-east Asia.

West Irian

Papua New Guinea

27

China

China is a huge country and more people live there than anywhere else in the world. Most Chinese people work on farms or in factories.

Beautiful silk has been made in China for centuries. The silkworm spins the threads which are woven into cloth.

Rice is a very important crop. It needs a hot climate and lots of water and is grown in fields called paddy fields.

flag of China

Mongolia

Desert

North Korea

Peking

Tianjin

Seoul
South Korea

China

R. Huang Ho

R. Changjiang/Yangtze

Shanghai

Taiwan

Hong Kong

The Great Wall of China was built over 2,000 years ago to keep out enemies. It is more than 2,000 kilometres long.

The giant panda is becoming very rare and is specially protected. It eats mainly bamboo shoots.

tea   rice   fishing   oil industry   coal   wheat or cereal

Japan

Japan is made up of four big islands and hundreds of small ones. Many Japanese live in the cities.

flag of Japan

Japan is known throughout the world for its industry.

Tokyo is the capital city and is always crowded with people and traffic.

Kite flying is a popular traditional pastime in Japan.

Hokkaido

Sapporo

Hanshu

Mt. Fujiyama

Tokyo

Yokohama

Nagoya

Kyoto

Osaka

Shikoku

Kyushu

Fishing is vital to Japan for food and for trade.

rice   fishing

New Zealand

New Zealanders are very successful farmers. They keep mostly sheep and cows.

Kiwis are small birds which cannot fly. They are found only in New Zealand.

In North Island steam and boiling water shoots out of the ground from hot springs which are called geysers.

The first people to live in New Zealand were Maoris. Their traditions are still a part of life today. Nearly all the Maoris live in North Island.

flag of New Zealand

Auckland

North Island

Wellington

Pacific Ocean

South Island

Christchurch

coal   fruit   wheat or cereal   fishing

Stewart Island

31

Australia

Australia is a huge country with big contrasts between its modern cities, wild bush land and large sheep farms. Some farms are so remote that the children do not go to school but have special lessons on two-way radios.

flag of Australia

Great Sandy Desert

Gibson Desert

Great Vic

Perth

Aborigines were the first inhabitants of Australia.

Wool is an important product. Sheep shearers use modern processes—but it is still very hard work.

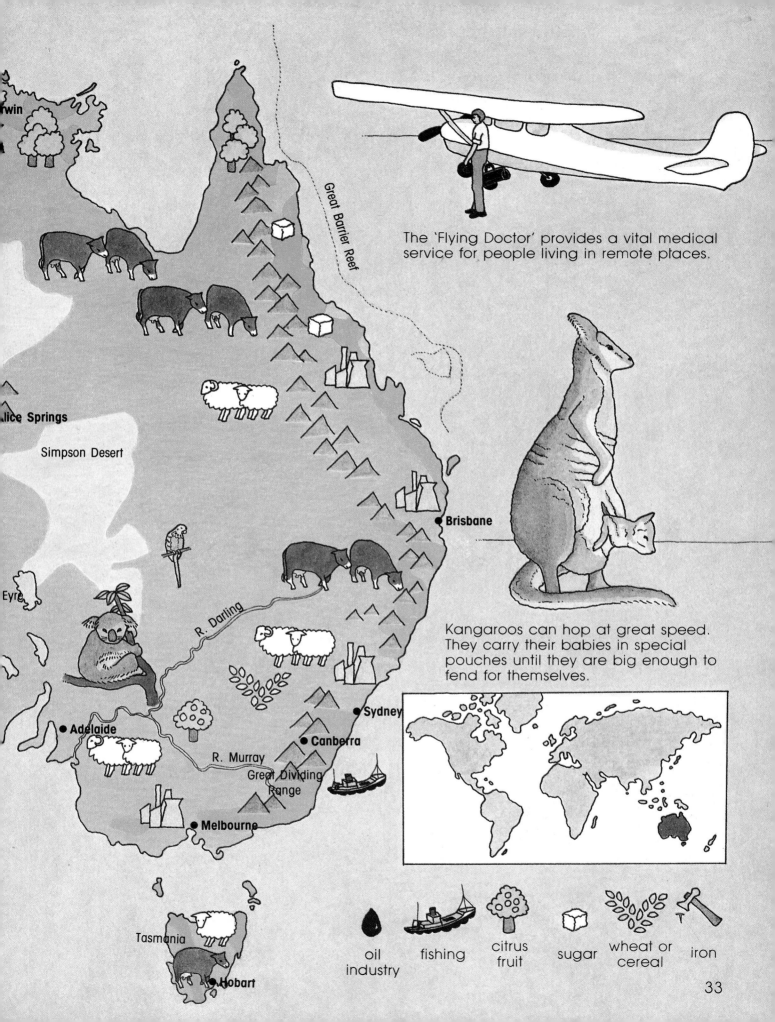

The 'Flying Doctor' provides a vital medical service for people living in remote places.

Kangaroos can hop at great speed. They carry their babies in special pouches until they are big enough to fend for themselves.

twin

Alice Springs

Simpson Desert

Great Barrier Reef

Eyre

R. Darling

● **Brisbane**

● **Adelaide**

R. Murray

Great Dividing Range

● **Sydney**

● **Canberra**

● **Melbourne**

Tasmania

● **Hobart**

oil industry

fishing

citrus fruit

sugar

wheat or cereal

iron

North America

Many people of different nations have explored and settled in North America. It has some of the biggest farms in the world and many exciting cities.

In Canada lumberjacks cut down trees for timber.

Greenland

Atlantic Ocean

Hudson Bay

Arctic Ocean

Canada

Alaska

flag of Canada

The Statue of Liberty welcomes all the people who come to New York.

New York City

Washington D.C.

Ottawa

Great Lakes

Chicago

Mississippi

New Orleans

United States of America

Missouri River

Denver

Rocky Mountains

San Francisco

Los Angeles

flag of the United States

American Indian tribes were the first people to live in North America. Many now live in special areas called reservations.

Disneyland is a popular place for everyone to visit.

Cowboys look after the great cattle ranches of the West.

grapes

citrus fruit

maize

cotton

gold

wheat or cereal

fruit

coal

oil

industry

35

Central America

Central America has large forests, where parrots and monkeys live, and high mountains. Most people work on farms.

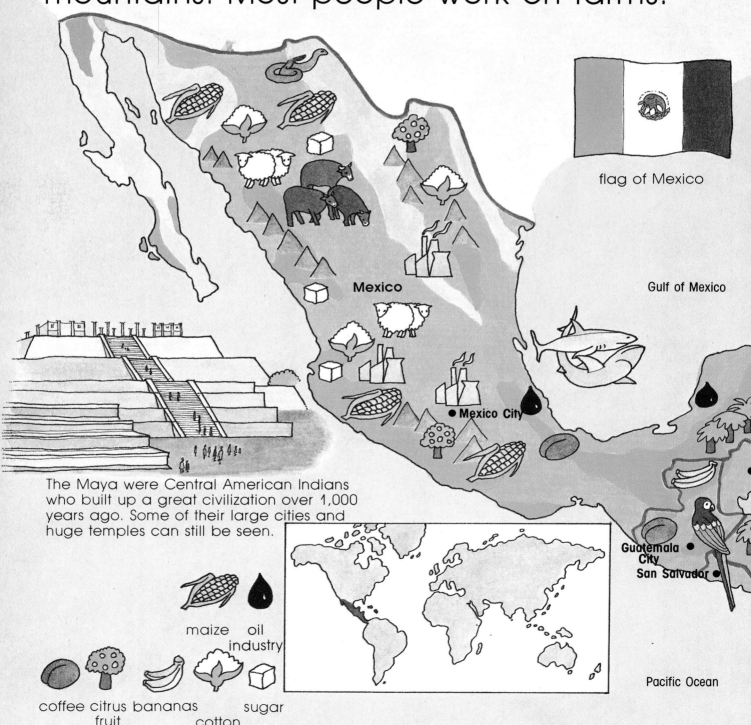

flag of Mexico

Mexico

Gulf of Mexico

Mexico City

The Maya were Central American Indians who built up a great civilization over 1,000 years ago. Some of their large cities and huge temples can still be seen.

Guatemala City

San Salvador

maize   oil
         industry

coffee citrus bananas   sugar
        fruit   cotton

Pacific Ocean

36

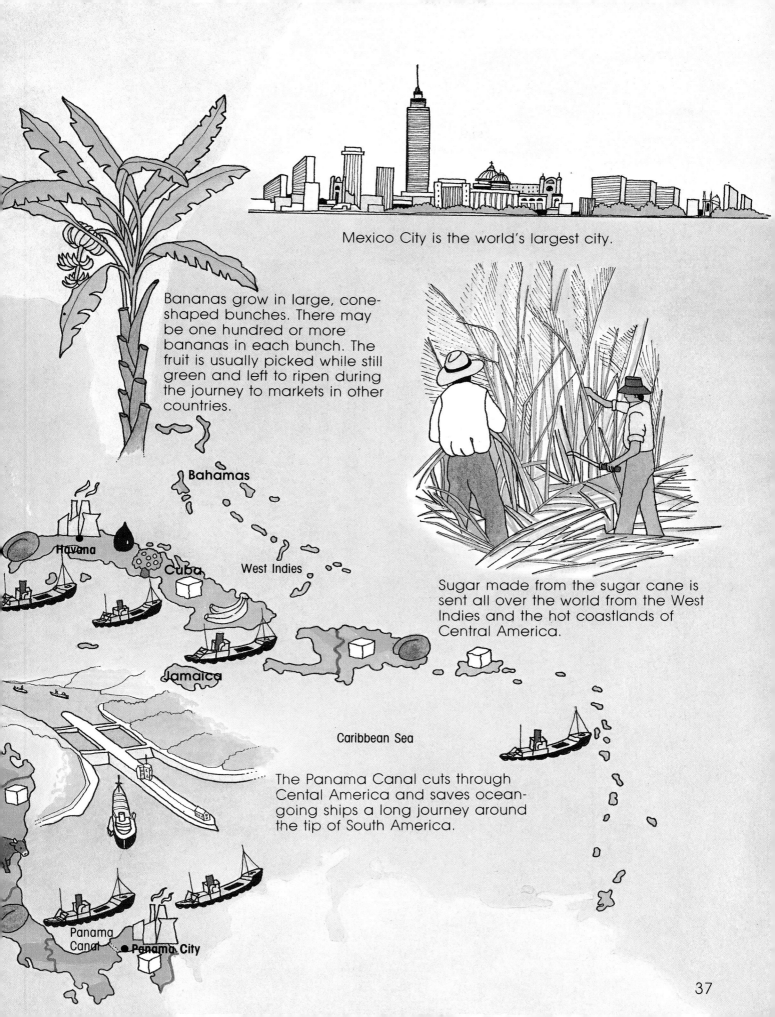

Mexico City is the world's largest city.

Bananas grow in large, cone-shaped bunches. There may be one hundred or more bananas in each bunch. The fruit is usually picked while still green and left to ripen during the journey to markets in other countries.

Sugar made from the sugar cane is sent all over the world from the West Indies and the hot coastlands of Central America.

Bahamas

Havana

Cuba

West Indies

Jamaica

Caribbean Sea

The Panama Canal cuts through Cental America and saves ocean-going ships a long journey around the tip of South America.

Panama Canal

Panama City

South America

South America is hot in the north and cold in the south. Some Indians still live in the large rain forests but many people work on large farms looking after sheep and cows. Coffee is a very important crop in Brazil.

The berries of the coffee tree are picked and roasted to make beans.

flag of Brazil

Caracas
Venezuela
Guyana
Surinam
French Guiana
Brazil
R. Amazon
Bogotá
Colombia
Quito
Ecuador
Peru

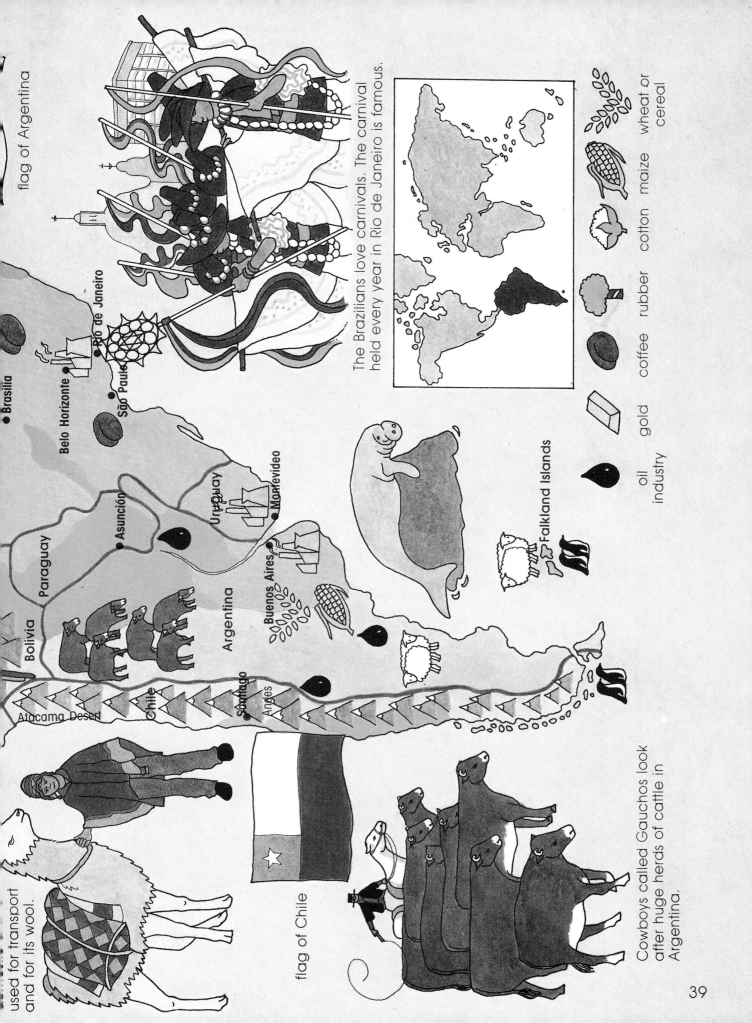

flag of Argentina

The Brazilians love carnivals. The carnival held every year in Rio de Janeiro is famous.

● Brasília

Belo Horizonte

São Paulo

● Rio de Janeiro

wheat or cereal

maize

cotton

rubber

coffee

gold

oil industry

Falkland Islands

Paraguay

Asunción

Uruguay

Montevideo

Bolivia

Buenos Aires

Argentina

Chile

Santiago

Andes

Atacama Desert

flag of Chile

used for transport and for its wool.

Cowboys called Gauchos look after huge herds of cattle in Argentina.

39

Africa

There are many countries in the continent of Africa. The biggest desert in the world, the Sahara, separates the north and the south. There are also large rivers, mountains, forests and lots of wild animals.

An oasis is a place in the desert where there is water. Plants can grow and people can settle there.

The Masai are an East African people who keep herds of cattle.

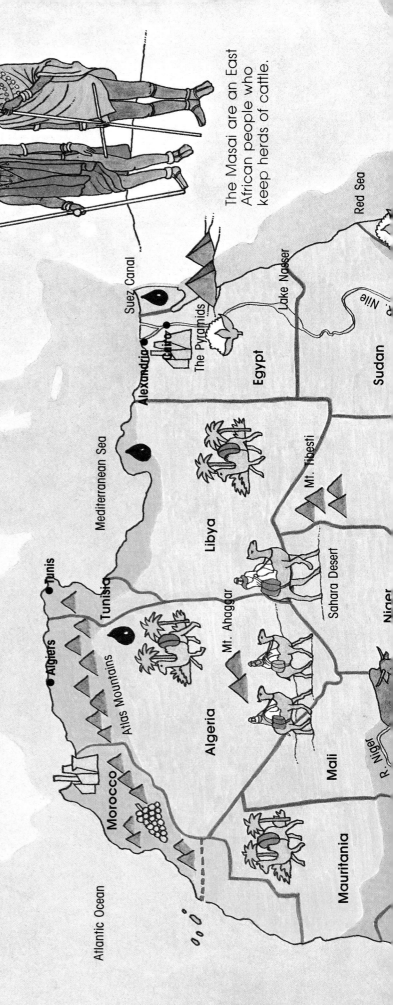

Suez Canal

Alexandria

Cairo

The Pyramids

Egypt

Lake Nasser

R. Nile

Red Sea

Sudan

Mediterranean Sea

Libya

Mt. Tibesti

Tunis

Tunisia

Mt. Ahaggar

Sahara Desert

Niger

Algiers

Atlas Mountains

Algeria

Mali

R. Niger

Morocco

Mauritania

Atlantic Ocean

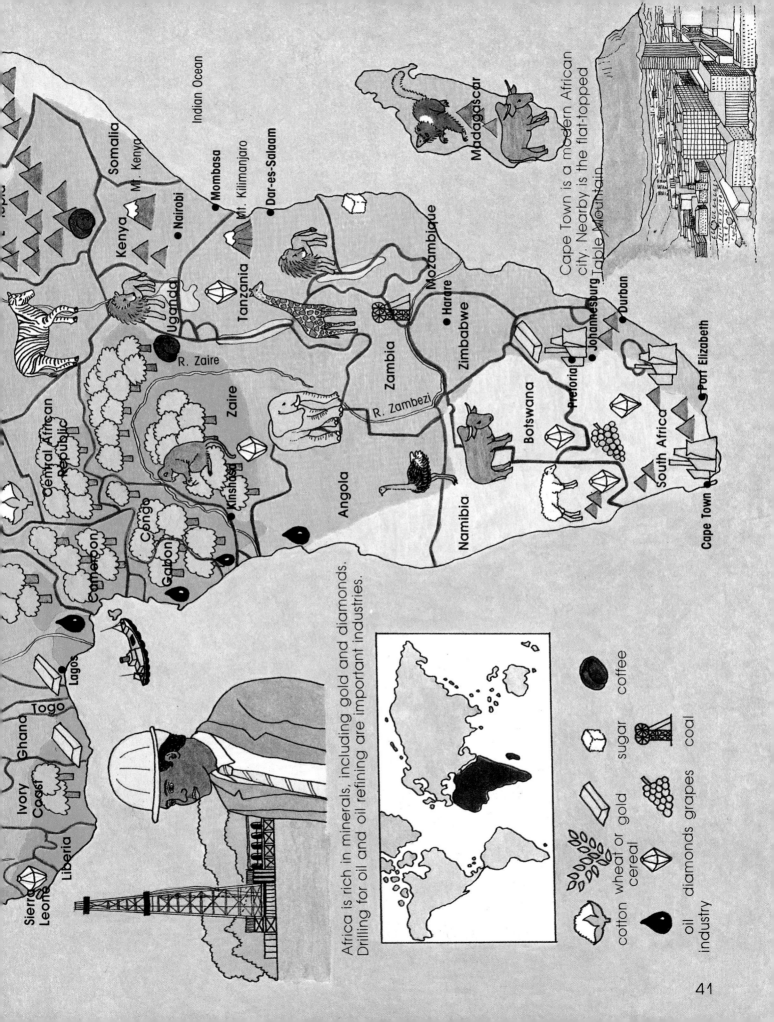

Indian Ocean

Somalia
Mt. Kenya
Kenya
Nairobi
Mombasa
Mt. Kilimanjaro
Dar-es-Salaam
Tanzania
Uganda
R. Zaire
Zaire
Central African Republic
Cameroon
Congo
Gabon
Kinshasa
Angola
Namibia
Botswana
Zambia
R. Zambezi
Zimbabwe
Harare
Mozambique
Madagascar

Sierra Leone
Liberia
Ivory Coast
Ghana
Togo
Lagos

Johannesburg
Pretoria
Durban
South Africa
Port Elizabeth
Cape Town

Cape Town is a modern African city. Nearby is the flat-topped Table Mountain

Africa is rich in minerals, including gold and diamonds. Drilling for oil and oil refining are important industries.

coffee
sugar
coal
cotton
wheat or cereal
gold
grapes
diamonds
oil
industry

41

The World is Round

Although we have looked at flat maps, the world is really round.

It is a good idea to imagine the world as an orange. If you peel the skin and open it out flat, you can show all parts of the world at the same time,

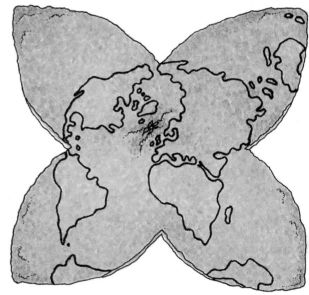

or the skin can be cut into pieces so that a country or group of countries is on each piece.

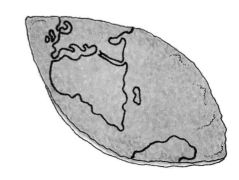

A map of the world is a picture of the world's **round** surface on a **flat** piece of paper.

The earth depends upon the sun shining on it to keep it light and warm.

If we take a torch and imagine it is the sun and shine it on to the orange, it looks like this:

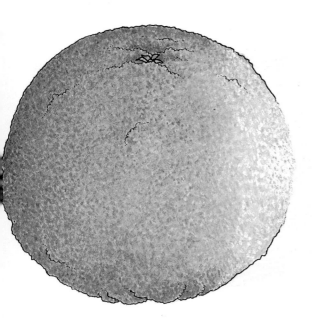

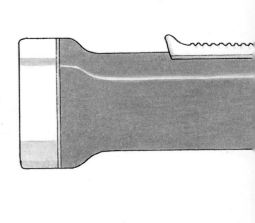

The middle of the orange is most brightly lit and the top and the bottom of the orange do not get much light. This is partly because the light has farther to go to reach the top and bottom of the orange. In the same way, the middle of the world gets more sunlight so it is much hotter, but because the earth is always spinning, different places get light and heat at different times.

There is an imaginary line around the middle of the earth, called the equator. The top and bottom points of the earth are called the North and South Poles.

North and South Poles

If you travelled from the equator to the North Pole in a straight line you would get colder and colder as you moved away from the equator. At the North Pole it would be very, very cold indeed. Similarly, travelling south from the equator you would at last reach the South Pole where the temperature is again always below freezing point.

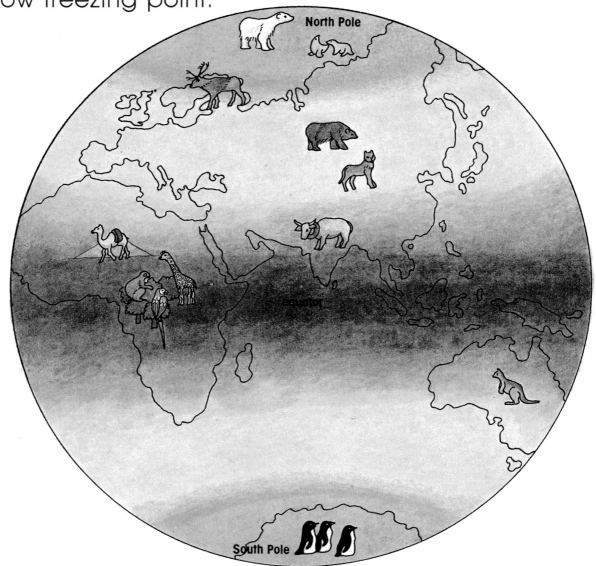

On your journey the scenery would also change because the plants and animals live in the temperatures they like best.

From a spaceship, the area around the North Pole, called the Arctic, would look like this:

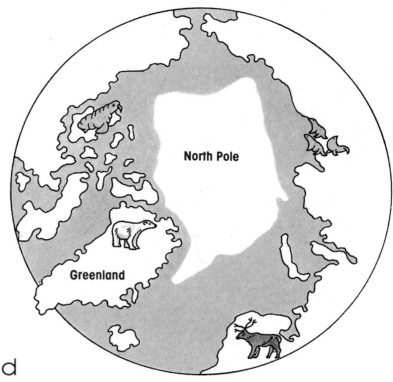

These areas of the world are very cold.

The area around the South Pole, called Antarctica, would look like this:

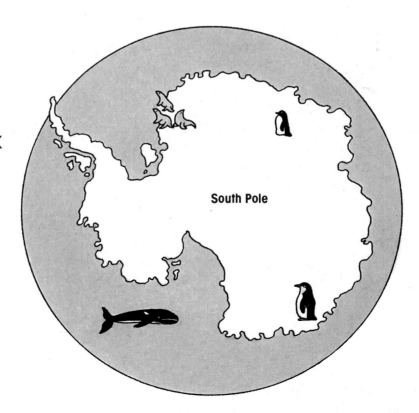